Table of Contents

Executive Summary

This document is the second biennial summary and progress report requested by the Federal Ocean Acidification Research and Monitoring Act of 2009 (FOARAM Act). The FOARAM Act specifies that the Subcommittee on Ocean Science and Technology (SOST) shall transmit a biennial report to the Committee on Commerce, Science, and Transportation of the Senate and the Committee on Science and Technology and the Committee on Natural Resources of the House of Representatives that includes:

(A.) a summary of Federally funded ocean acidification research and monitoring activities, including the budget for each of these activities; and

(B.) an analysis of the progress made toward achieving the goals and priorities for the interagency research plan developed by the Subcommittee under section 12405.

This report summarizes Federal activities related to ocean acidification for fiscal years 2010 and 2011. Activities are classified as having either a primary focus on ocean acidification or being "contributing" activities, in that they were designed for other purposes but clearly provide information useful for understanding ocean acidification.

In 2010, Federal agencies spent approximately $29 million on activities with a primary focus on ocean acidification and an additional $9 million on contributing studies. In 2011, funding was approximately $21 million for primary studies and $8 million for contributing studies. This difference reflects NSF's biennial funding cycle for research proposals related to ocean acidification. Activities funded during the period of this report include monitoring of ocean chemistry and biological impacts; research to understand species specific and ecosystem responses to ocean acidification; biogeochemical and ecosystem modeling; technology development; assessment of socioeconomic impacts from ocean acidification; education and outreach activities; data management and integration;

and other activities. Activities with a primary focus on ocean acidification were directed at understanding biological, species, and ecosystem responses. Another large effort was directed at monitoring of ocean chemistry and biological impacts. Contributing activities largely focused on monitoring and on species and ecosystem responses to ocean acidification.

A Strategic Research Plan for Ocean Acidification, as required by the FOARAM Act, has been developed and is under review with anticipated delivery in summer 2013. The Subcommittee on Ocean Science and Technology (SOST) is conferring with domestic and international scientific advisory groups concerned with ocean acidification to ensure that the plan is well coordinated with non-government scientists and is informed by the latest scientific knowledge. Also, as required by the FOARAM Act, the NOAA Ocean Acidification Program was established with the hiring of Director Elizabeth Jewett in May 2011.

Introduction

The Federal Ocean Acidification Research and Monitoring Act of 2009 (FOARAM Act, Public Law 111-11, Subtitle D) directed the Subcommittee on Ocean Science and Technology (SOST), which is governed by the Committee on Environment, Natural Resources, and Sustainability of the National Science and Technology Council, to create an Interagency Working Group on Ocean Acidification (IWG-OA). Section 12404(c) of the FOARAM Act further specifies that the SOST will transmit a biennial report to the Committee on Commerce, Science, and Transportation of the Senate, and the Committee on Science and Technology and Committee on Natural Resources of the House of Representatives, which includes:

(A.) a summary of federally funded ocean acidification research and

monitoring activities, including the budget for each of these activities; and

(B.) an analysis of the progress made toward achieving the goals and priorities for the

interagency research plan developed by the Subcommittee under section 12405.

This constitutes the second biennial summary and progress report of the SOST IWG- OA. The IWG-OA was chartered by SOST in October 2009, is chaired by the National Oceanic and Atmospheric Administration (NOAA), and includes additional representatives from NOAA, the National Aeronautics and Space Administration (NASA), National Science Foundation (NSF), U.S. Geological Survey (USGS), Environmental Protection Agency (EPA), Bureau of Ocean Energy Management (BOEM), Department of State (DOS), U.S. Navy, and U.S. Fish and Wildlife Service (FWS). The group meets to coordinate ocean acidification activities across the Federal Government and has made significant progress toward meeting the goals of the FOARAM Act.

The report is organized into seven main sections corresponding to the categories of information in the draft strategic plan for ocean acidification research and monitoring, plus one additional section for those items that cannot be adequately described by the other seven. Each section contains an overview of the activities conducted within that category by Federal Agencies in fiscal years 2010 and 2011. Appendix 1 provides a summary of individual agency ocean acidification research and monitoring activities, including the budget for each of these activities. Activities are classified as either having a primary focus on ocean acidification or being "contributing" activities, in that they were designed for other purposes but clearly provide information useful for understanding ocean acidification.

Section 1. Monitoring of ocean chemistry and biological impacts associated with ocean acidification at selected coastal and open-ocean monitoring stations, including satellite-based monitoring to characterize marine ecosystems, changes in marine productivity, and changes in ocean chemistry.

To understand the progress of ocean acidification in open-ocean and coastal environments and the impacts on marine ecosystems it is necessary to employ a coordinated, multi-disciplinary approach to observations and modeling. In 2010 and 2011, EPA, BOEM, NOAA, NSF, and USGS supported studies that addressed monitoring ocean chemistry or biological impacts associated with ocean acidification. In 2010, approximately $5,839,000 was spent on monitoring related to ocean acidification and approximately $5,110,000 was spent on activities that were not specifically termed ocean acidification studies but contributed to ocean acidification monitoring studies. In 2011, $6,425,000 was spent on monitoring related to ocean acidification and approximately $4,887,000 was spent on studies that contributed to monitoring studies.

Marine Ecosystems

In 2010 and 2011, numerous studies focused on monitoring ocean acidification in the context of its effects on marine ecosystems. Agency activities included, for example, large-scale efforts to study the impacts of ocean acidification on corals surrounding Puerto Rico, Florida, and the Pacific Islands.

NOAA-supported research programs on this topic were focused primarily on the effects of ocean acidification on corals and their associated ecosystems. These studies addressed the impacts of ocean acidification in a geological context to quantify baseline variability in coral growth and seawater pH, while assessing the historical response of coral ecosystems to increased atmospheric carbon dioxide (CO_2). Lab experiments and model studies explored the effects of ocean acidification on natural coral-reef ecosystems in the Pacific Islands by investigating past and current calcification rates of reef-building corals. To better understand the threats to coral reefs posed by acidification, and to support longer-term development of adaptive management and conservation strategies, Pacific Island studies established baseline observations of the spatial patterns and temporal variability of seawater carbonate chemistry and associated biogeochemical processes, including calcification of coral reefs across key gradients of habitat type, benthic composition, oceanographic conditions, and human uses. NOAA also funded research projects to evaluate the effects of warming and acidification on vulnerable early-life stages of threatened Caribbean reef-building corals.

Under its Environmental Studies Program, the Bureau of Oceans and Energy Management (BOEM) is contributing to the knowledge of ocean acidification through research taking place in the Arctic Ocean and the Gulf of Mexico. Through this effort, NOAA is conducting ocean research to provide science to support decision-making regarding oil and gas leasing of the Outer Continental Shelf. BOEM scientists and partners are engaged in research in the Chukchi Sea, investigating the current status of regional ecosystems and their vulnerability to acidification. Furthermore, USGS studies are providing information regarding ocean acidification impacts on coral metabolism, calcification rates, and interactions between corals and their algal symbionts.

Changes in Marine Productivity

During the period of this report, USGS programs were aimed at determining the baselines and thresholds of various coral reef communities to changes in the partial pressure of carbon dioxide (pCO_2), calcium saturation state, and ocean acidification by measuring coral metabolic and calcification rates.

Changes in Ocean Chemistry

The NOAA Ocean Acidification Monitoring Program along North American coastlines (Atlantic, Gulf of Mexico, Pacific, and Alaska) and open ocean focused on mapping and monitoring the distribution of key indicators of ocean acidification including CO_2, pH, and carbonate mineral saturation states. The overarching goal of the program was to determine trends in ocean acidification and provide information for use in addressing acidification issues. The monitoring effort was conducted with sensors deployed from a variety of platforms, including moorings, ships of opportunity, and more detailed hydrographic research cruises along U.S. coasts. Results from these studies have provided seasonal and inter-annual assessments of changes in carbon chemistry.

Monitoring efforts in the Bering Strait and off the coast of Florida and in the Arctic Ocean, funded by NSF and USGS respectively, utilized a network of repeat hydrographic surveys, time-series stations, and volunteer observing ships. These efforts provided a strong observational foundation of the carbonate chemistry needed to address ocean acidification in open-ocean and coastal waters.

Section 2. Research to understand the species-specific physiological responses of marine organisms to ocean acidification and impacts on marine food webs of ocean acidification, and to develop environmental and ecological indices that track marine ecosystem responses to ocean acidification.

Marine-biological processes can be affected by ocean acidification due to changes in pH or fluctuations in the concentrations of dissolved CO_2, bicarbonate ion, or carbonate ion. Nearly every major biological function has been shown to respond to these chemical changes in seawater, including rates of photosynthesis, respiration, growth, calcification, reproduction, and recruitment. NSF, NOAA, USGS, NASA, and EPA spent approximately $20,432,000 on activities directly related to the effects of ocean acidification on marine organisms in 2010, and $11,449,000 in 2011. Funding was higher in 2010 than 2011 because NSF only funds ocean acidification proposals every other year. Roughly $2,180,000 was spent on other activities that were not specifically termed ocean-acidification studies but contributed to ocean acidification research in 2010, and an additional $1,753,000 was spent in 2011.

Biology of impacted species

Federal agency activities in 2010 and 2011 that focused on studying the effects of ocean acidification on calcification and other physiological processes were diverse, spanning molecular and physiological functions including impacts on growth, reproduction, and survival.

Several scientific studies supported by NSF measured the effects of changing seawater pH and associated carbon parameters on coral physiology, calcification, gene expression, and immune responses; pH changes in estuarine systems and effects on organisms with $CaCO_3$ exoskeletons; and effects of increasing pH on fish development. EPA also supported studies in 2011 that examined the impacts of ocean acidification on the demography of marine mysids and effects on growth and food consumption by juvenile winter flounder.

NOAA-supported research focused on assessing physiological effects on living marine resources and the resulting effects on ecosystems. The three northern NOAA Fisheries Science Centers (Alaska, Northwest, and Northeast) are coordinating their efforts on studies to investigate the impacts of ocean acidification on living marine resources.

USGS supported studies of the effects of ocean acidification on coral health and coral reef degradation, as well as monitoring of coralline algae that form "crusts" of calcium carbonate. Studies started in 2008 on the effects of lowered pH and higher CO_2 values in seawater on photosynthesis and respiration of different tropical and subtropical benthic organisms are continuing. Additionally, BOEM, NOAA, and USGS are working together to research deep-water coral communities, related ecosystems, and the microbial communities associated with them.

NASA continued funding satellite research to investigate ocean color. Ocean color can be used to measure particulate inorganic carbon (PIC), biogenic silica, and pCO_2. NASA also funded efforts to reduce uncertainty when measuring phytoplankton chlorophyll in the ocean. These efforts provide the foundation to observe physiological processes such as photosynthesis, evaluate phytoplankton health, and provide global datasets for modeling efforts that include ocean acidification. Much of this work also supports NASA's Earth Science carbon cycle science program.

Ecosystems and food webs

Marine food webs can be complex, and changes in one or more key species may have serious repercussions. Because ocean acidification has the potential to affect key species at the base of marine food webs, it has the potential to alter marine food webs up to and including fishery-species of interest. Further, decreases in calcium carbonate production may alter the structural fabric of some seafloor ecosystems by affecting hard-bottom habitats. Many marine plants and animals depend on the complex habitat provided by corals and other associated organisms in both tropical and cold-water systems. Oyster and clam beds, which provide critical habitat in temperate waters, may also be affected by decreased carbonate production.

NSF sponsored ocean acidification research on the effects of increased pCO_2 and decreased pH on photosynthesis, respiration, and growth in marine phytoplankton; physiological effects of pCO_2 on larvae development of benthic organisms; changes in the protist community structure with increased pCO_2 and temperature; and effects of iron availability on phytoplankton composition in water with reduced pH levels.

NASA continued funding regional and global-scale assessments of primary productivity and completed the Southern Ocean Gas Exchange Experiment, which focused on mechanisms of air-sea gas exchange (e.g., CO_2) in the Southern Ocean. NASA also funded ongoing research to identify and develop possible proxies for ocean acidification monitoring from satellite data, including studies to improve interpretation of fluorescence signals observable from space, and *in situ* platforms such as underwater gliders.

Calcification processes

Changes in the carbonate ion concentration in seawater affect the "saturation states" of the various calcium-carbonate minerals that are used by marine organisms to produce their shells or skeletons. The carbonate ion concentration of seawater decreases dramatically with ocean acidification and the resulting decrease in availability of carbonate ions may impact shell and skeletal formation of many organisms including corals, shellfish, sea urchins, and certain algae.

In 2010, NSF supported fundamental research to develop a global surface-ocean baseline for pH; evaluate the physical and biogeochemical processes involving carbonate minerals in the western Arctic Ocean; and characterize temporal and spatial variability in pH along the Pacific coast. NSF and NOAA also sponsored studies to determine the effects of and controls on seasonal hypoxia and acidification as well as the ramifications for shellfish and finfish. NASA funded research to evaluate different methodologies for discerning the impact of ocean acidification on calcifying plankton at basin scales.

Other marine chemical and physical attributes

The major nutrient cycles in the ocean, which include geological, chemical, physical, and biological processes, determine the availability of nutrients that support all ocean life, as well as the ability of the oceans to sequester CO_2 from the atmosphere. Ocean acidification has the potential to alter both chemical and biological processes that will affect nutrient and carbon cycles.

In 2010, NSF supported the documentation and understanding of how ocean acidification may affect the formation and sinking of organic and inorganic particles within the water column. USGS supported studies that evaluated coastal-carbon fluxes and submarine groundwater discharges, which act as additional causes of stress on coral reefs in addition to the stress they already experience due to ocean acidification. USGS also developed numerical modeling systems for the flow patterns and discharge rates to Biscayne Bay, which may provide insight into causes of ecosystem degradation.

NASA funded and completed field research to be utilized by the Impacts of Climate Change on the Eco-Systems and Chemistry of the Arctic Pacific Environment (ICESCAPE) field campaign. The goal of ICESCAPE is to determine the impact of climate change on the biogeochemistry and ecosystems of the Chukchi and Beaufort seas. ICESCAPE utilizes an interdisciplinary, cross-cutting approach to integrate field expeditions, modeling, and satellite remote sensing. Currently, ICESCAPE is analyzing observations to address the impacts of ocean acidification on Arctic ecosystems.

The historical record of ocean acidification on Earth

Studies supported by USGS and NSF in 2010 and 2011 compared historic calcification rates with current rates to inform modeling of future rates. USGS continued supporting work initiated in 2009, which focused on the synthesis of historical, physical, and chemical records at shellfish-bed sites within Florida to provide a regional view of ocean acidification. NSF sponsored studies to examine ocean acidification in the geologic record.

NSF and USGS supported the development of the use of boron isotopes and their ratio to calcium as a proxy to determine seawater pH. This technique can be applied to samples from marine sediments, drill sections from coral reefs, and preserved exoskeletons of gastropods to ascertain environmental conditions in Earth's history. The method has further potential to reflect glacial/interglacial changes of surface seawater pH and atmospheric CO_2 levels.

Section 3. Modeling to predict changes in the ocean carbon cycle as a function of carbon dioxide and atmosphere-induced changes in temperature, ocean circulation, biogeochemistry, and ecosystem and terrestrial inputs, and modeling to determine impacts on marine ecosystems and individual marine organisms.

A wide variety of activities during 2010 and 2011 were associated with modeling the marine-carbon cycle and ocean acidification. Approximately \$882,000 was spent on activities directly related to ocean acidification modeling in 2010, and \$831,000 in 2011. Roughly \$1,176,000 was spent in 2010 on activities that were not specifically termed ocean acidification studies but contributed to ocean acidification modeling, and \$838,000 in 2011.

These contributing modeling efforts are expected to increase our understanding of ocean acidification through the improved depiction of land-air-sea carbon coupling, understanding carbon fluxes in hydrologic and geologic processes, and defining spatial distributions and fluxes of carbon (i.e., sources and sinks of carbon), production of CO_2 from photosynthesis and respiration, and oceanic carbon cycling. Additional modeling of linkages between solubility of nutrients and carbon sources and sinks will help improve future modeling efforts of ocean acidification.

Physico-chemical change

USGS is supporting modeling of historical and future changes in the ocean carbon cycle through the use of boron as a proxy from coral cores. These data are being used to model ecosystem change over historic and geologic time scales. In 2011, NSF sponsored studies using observationally based analyses of past mechanisms of transport for anthropogenic CO_2 in the ocean that can be used to project future transport and deposition.

NOAA supported projects to investigate effects of hypoxia and associated day-night swings in pH in shallow waters. These accompanying swings in pH may exacerbate the effects of hypoxia, and the combination of these factors may lead to effects more severe than those predicted by lab experiments that examined the effects of low oxygen in isolation.

In 2010 and 2011, NOAA also funded the development of algorithms for the California Current along U.S. west coast intended to be applied to legacy data sets like those collected by the National Marine Fisheries Service in their annual transects. When successful, these applications can expand our historical knowledge of ocean acidification in certain regions.

NASA funded research to develop methods for predicting coastal surface-water pCO_2 using remote-sensing data. Improved methodology will increase our basic understanding of how satellites monitoring ocean color can be used to estimate ocean acidity regionally and globally, and also will provide quantitative information on carbon cycling.

Ecological/Biological Impacts

NSF supported programs that contributed to the basic understanding of the effects of ocean acidification. For example, efforts along the Alaskan North Slope examined the link between iron solubility, speciation, marine productivity, and carbon sequestration to determine the possible impacts of climate change and ocean acidification on Alaskan marine ecosystems, with possible implications for other regions. EPA also supported modeling efforts in 2011, focusing on the eco-systemic and biological impacts of ocean acidification using inverse demographic techniques.

NOAA supported the reorganization of a Puget Sound ecosystem model, which will improve the ability to predict the response of the Puget Sound food web to ocean acidification. In addition, NOAA is engaged in investigating the dynamics of the Dungeness crab under various ocean acidification scenarios using a species life-cycle modeling framework. This work will also aid future forecasting of the Alaskan king crab.

NOAA's program to evaluate the effect of ocean acidification on marine resources in the northeast U.S. continental shelf region integrates the observational and experimental data generated from ecosystem and population models that are currently used by scientists assessing living marine resources. This program will allow for the effects of ocean acidification to be communicated to managers in the same form of scientific models and assessments that they use now NASA supported modeling of ocean acidification within the greater Caribbean. This work utilized seawater carbonate-system data acquired from ships of opportunity to refine algorithms derived from satellite data. These algorithms are being used to compute saturation state and other carbon properties of the ocean that are useful in monitoring, research, and modeling of changing ocean acidity and the impacts of changing acidity on the ocean's ecosystems.

Section 4. Technology development and standardization of carbonate chemistry measurements on moorings and autonomous floats.

Research needs and priorities identified in the FOARAM Act, through agency planning, and in the 2010 National Research Council report, *Ocean Acidification: A National Strategy to Meet the Challenges of a Changing Ocean*, point to the necessity of improved instrumentation, sensors, and methods to support long-term observations, systematic ocean surveys, and the development of experimental systems to investigate organism and ecosystem responses to ocean acidification. Approximately $1,160,000 was spent on activities directly related to technology development for ocean acidification in

2010, and $626,000 in 2011. A further $306,000 was spent on activities that were not specifically for ocean acidification technology development, but contributed to it, in 2010; no additional money was spent in 2011 on contributing activities.

USGS, cooperating with NOAA and universities, supported the refinement and standardization of methods for measuring carbon parameters and calcification in coral reef systems as part of an effort to understand the metabolic function of reef systems. USGS also supported the development of flow-through systems for the rapid measurement of CO_2 levels in water, which will serve both marine and freshwater uses.

NOAA ocean acidification technology activities in 2010 and 2011 focused on the development of observing gliders, a dissolved inorganic carbon sensor, and methods for determining variations in ocean acidification and ecosystem response in coral reefs. The systems combine wave-powered autonomous surface vehicles (unmanned observing systems that harness ocean wave energy to provide essentially limitless propulsion while solar panels continually replenish the batteries used to power the electronic observing systems) with instruments to take pCO_2 (air and water), pH, temperature, and salinity measurements. The vehicles were deployed to evaluate how conditions varied between research cruises. The glider data are used to assess the temporal variability of upwelling and hypoxia on the Oregon shelf. Researchers can then use these data to create algorithms that can be applied to predict pH and aragonite saturation. A successful and robust mobile system can be applied to establish the broader carbonate-system-chemistry dynamics across reef systems, and will also assist in identifying sites for future mooring deployments.

NOAA invested resources in 2010 and 2011 in the development of a new sensor for deployment on moored observing platforms for the measurement of dissolved inorganic carbon. Given the limitations inherent in using pH and pCO_2 to constrain the carbonate system, it is critically important to develop additional, robust sensors for measuring a third parameter. The sensor is still in the experimental phase of development.

NOAA also supported programs to investigate the physical and biogeochemical processes controlling temporal variability in ocean acidification. Efforts were focused on the Conch Reef in Florida. The goal of this program is to advance the development of an integrated set of high-precision, *in situ* measurements, using state-of-the-art cabled instrumentation that can examine the influence of benthic processes on local carbonate chemistry in real time.

NSF is supporting a variety of new measurement technologies. The Agency supported efforts to develop instrumentation that would allow researchers to control and adjust seawater composition in multiple aquaria simultaneously and vary the composition when needed, for use in ocean acidification experiments in closed systems. NOAA has invested in similar equipment development for its fishery-science laboratories. NSF also funded research to develop a micro-rosette sensor for totally dissolved inorganic carbon to be used by autonomous float observing systems.

The standard method for measuring coral reef calcification requires knowledge of the alkalinity differences between the reef and the offshore source water, as well as the residence time of the water over the reef. Gathering this information is expensive and time-consuming. With NSF support, a method using an isotope of boron is being developed to estimate the residence time from a simple set of inexpensive measurements. The use of boron isotopes as a proxy for seawater pH was also supported by USGS and NSF (see Section 2, *The record of Earth system history regarding ocean acidification*).

NASA continued to support the development, assessment, and commercialization of a biogeochemical profiling float for ocean carbon studies. The float is designed to incorporate a suite of instruments to remotely quantify components of the carbon cycle, such as primary production, using miniaturized optical sensors on ARGO-type floats, and it will serve as a platform for new sensors of the dissolved-carbonate system.

Section 5. Assessment of socioeconomic impacts of ocean acidification and development of adaptation and mitigation strategies to conserve marine organisms and marine ecosystems.

From an economic perspective, the ocean and coastal environments provide valuable goods and services. The "goods" refer to marine resources such as fish, shellfish, and other organisms and items that are harvested for food and other consumer products. Some of the "services" include the cycling and sequestration of carbon, maintaining biodiversity, and providing opportunities for recreation. The human activities that rely on these goods and services are often intertwined with the social fabric of coastal communities and tribal groups. Understanding the interactions between the oceans and human systems is critical to protecting environmental public health. In 2010 and 2011 the NOAA and the EPA allocated funding for socioeconomic studies related to ocean acidification, with all funding allocated for primary research programs. Approximately $157,000 was spent on activities directly related to the development of integrated assessment models in 2010, and $269,000 was spent on these activities in 2011.

NOAA has been supporting the development of a model in Alaska to estimate the economic impacts of ocean acidification's effects on the Alaskan king crab. EPA has supported the development of biophysical models and new methodologies to determine the economic and intrinsic value of coral reefs and shellfish. The Coral Mortality and Bleaching

Output (COMBO) model is used by managers, conservationists, and biologists to predict the effects of climate change and ocean acidification on coral reefs at local-to-regional scales, and new economic valuation approaches have been applied to estimate damages. The EPA's National Center for Environmental Economics (NCEE) is conducting research to assess the economic impacts of ocean acidification on U.S. mollusk fisheries, for inclusion in monetary estimates of damages from greenhouse gas emissions.

Section 6. Education/Outreach on ocean acidification.

Engaging stakeholders and the public is an important aspect of addressing the implications of ocean acidification. Exchanging information, education, and outreach can occur through multiple types of media, including websites, workshops, and publications. Workshops and special sessions at professional meetings have been conducted to engage the scientific community and to provide input for planning. Approximately $349,000 was spent on activities directly related to ocean acidification outreach in 2010, and $392,000 in 2011. An additional $50,000 was spent on activities that were not specifically termed ocean acidification studies but contributed to ocean acidification outreach in 2010, and no additional money was spent on contributing programs in 2011.

The State Department has been involved with various international activities relevant to ocean acidification. In the 2010 United Nations General Assembly Oceans and Law of the Sea Resolution, the United States supported language expressing concern over ocean acidification and encouraged further research on the matter. At the United Nations Informal Consultative Process on Oceans and Law of the Sea in 2011, the United States stated the importance of increased international collaboration and data sharing on observations and research in order to better understand and anticipate the effects of ocean acidification. Advisory councils representing NOAA's 13 national marine sanctuaries passed resolutions and made recommendations encouraging regional and national coordination and support in research, education, outreach, and other activities related to ocean acidification.

NOAA has developed displays and activities concerning ocean acidification and how it may impact the Puget Sound ecosystem at the Seattle Aquarium. They have incorporated new concepts in ocean acidification research and have made advances in how to best convey the complex chemistry, physiology, and ecology that underlie ocean acidification and make it an issue for concern. Recognizing the need for more researchers who will focus on ocean acidification, NOAA has engaged in the mentorship of young scientists by hosting undergraduate interns during their mid-winter breaks from school. In addition, NOAA funded daylong educator workshops in Florida where more than 80 educators were trained.

NOAA also developed an ocean acidification educational website to provide a one-stop site on ocean acidification that included presentations, demonstrations, simulations, classroom activities, and science papers. Furthermore, NOAA developed and produced an ocean acidification educational DVD, which has been presented at National Science Teachers Association and other national educator conferences. During this time NOAA also created a publically available database of the estimated vulnerabilities of northwest coast species to the direct effects of ocean acidification, and a classroom module using ocean acidification data was built into five lesson plans hosted on a dedicated teacher/student web interface. Finally, NOAA has trained many undergraduate students in ocean acidification research methodologies through the Hollings Scholar Program.

USGS presents research activities and findings through its website, particularly the Sound Waves newsletter and other outreach mechanisms. NSF continues to sponsor the

Symposium on The Ocean in a High-CO_2 World. The symposium aims to attract the world's leading scientists to discuss the impacts of ocean acidification on marine organisms, ecosystems, and biogeochemical cycles, as well as to identify priorities for future research. It also covers socioeconomic consequences of ocean acidification, including policy and management implications.

NASA continued to support scientific research awards for projects seeeking to enhance the public and educational outreach on subjects related to carbon-cycle science, interdisciplinary science, and ocean acidification.

Section 7. Data management and integration

Data management and integration are critical to the success and impact of any research program. Data must be shared and integrated across disciplinary boundaries, drawing marine-biological data together with oceanographic data and providing intelligible information to social scientists, planners, educators, and the general public. Data must also be shared and integrated across organizational boundaries, blending data from diverse systems that were created to address distinct mission goals. For example, data collected by the regional observing associations into the national U.S. Integrated Ocean Observing System (IOOS) provide easier and better access to this information by end users. Finally, data must be shared and integrated across data management technology boundaries that currently limit the interoperability between *in situ* observations and gridded fields such as satellite products, data synthesis products, and numerical model outputs.

NSF funded the Biological and Chemical Oceanography Data Management Office with approximately $75,000 in 2010 and $80,000 in 2011, contributing to ocean acidification data management. NOAA allocated approximately $100,000 in 2010 and approximately $256,000 in 2011 for activities directly related to the development of data management systems and data integration processes, including funding for a 2012 Ocean Acidification Integrated Data Management Workshop to bring together scientists and data managers from across NOAA and other federal agencies. The workshop's purpose was to determine the best way to share and integrate all ocean acidification data for easy public access and to accelerate research progress.

The ocean acidification data management system has begun to accommodate ocean acidification data from moored, cruise, and other observation efforts currently underway. The ocean acidification data management system will leverage current data systems that support the Surface Ocean Carbon Atlas, which brings together, in a common format, all publicly available surface-water data from the global oceans, including the Arctic, and the coastal seas. Responsibilities will include documentation, user assistance, and tools for analysis and visualization, as well as database management.

Section 8. Other ocean acidification research and monitoring activities

In addition to the specific monitoring, biological response, modeling, technology development, socioeconomic impact, education and outreach, and data management activities, funding has been allocated to develop programs, processes, and infrastructure to enable these core activities. In 2011, approximately $515,000 was spent on the development of the NOAA Ocean Acidification Program Office, including a National Research Council review of the Strategic Research Plan as called for by the FOARAM Act. In 2010 and 2011

NSF spent an additional $151,000 per year renovating laboratories for the purpose of improving ocean acidification research.

The NOAA Ocean Acidification Program (OAP) was established under SEC. 12406. of the FOARAM Act to oversee and coordinate research, monitoring, and other activities consistent with the strategic research and implementation plan developed by the IWG- OA. The OAP, together with the agency and interagency research efforts mentioned above, works to foster, coordinate, and direct: (A) interdisciplinary research among the ocean and atmospheric sciences and research and other activities to improve understanding of ocean acidification; (B) the establishment of a long-term monitoring program of ocean acidification utilizing existing global and national ocean-observing assets, adding instrumentation and sampling stations as appropriate to the aims of the research program; (C) research to identify and develop adaptation strategies and techniques for effectively conserving marine ecosystems as they cope with increased ocean acidification; (D) educational opportunities that encourage an interdisciplinary and international approach to exploring the impacts of ocean acidification; (E) national public outreach activities to improve the understanding of current scientific knowledge of ocean acidification and its impacts on marine resources; and (F) coordination of ocean acidification monitoring and impacts research with other appropriate international ocean science bodies such as the International Oceanographic Commission, the International Council for the Exploration of the Sea, and the North Pacific Marine Science Organization. A key part of the OAP's responsibility is to provide grants for critical research projects that explore the effects of ocean acidification on ecosystems and the socioeconomic impacts of increased ocean acidification that are relevant to the goals and priorities of the strategic research plan. The OAP incorporates a competitive merit-based process for awarding grants that may be conducted jointly with other participating agencies or under the National Oceanographic Partnership Program.

NSF awarded the University of South Florida funds to renovate their marine science laboratory. The College of Marine Science there has a strong research program with a focus on corals and ocean acidification issues. Similarly, NSF funded renovations to the marine science observing systems at the University of Maryland Center for Environmental Sciences, where researchers are helping develop the next generation of environmental observation systems. When mature, this technology will allow scientists to analyze data in near real-time and pass that information to policymakers and natural resource managers to improve environmental custody.

Under the Energy Independence and Security Act of 2007, USGS has significant responsibilities to develop scientifically-based methods for assessment of biologic and geologic carbon sequestration capacities and to perform a comprehensive nationwide resource assessment examining the full range of geothermal resources. As part of efforts to fulfill this responsibility, USGS chairs the newly formed interdisciplinary carbon committee of scientists and managers. The committee will develop a long-term strategy for comprehensive assessment of carbon-sequestration resources, including the potential for new carbon sequestration and for conservation and enhancement of existing carbon-storage systems.

Progress on the Strategic Research Plan for Ocean Acidification

The IWG-OA is developing the Strategic Research Plan for Ocean Acidification as required by the FOARAM Act, and a table of contents for the draft plan is provided below.

This draft plan is in the review process indicated in the FOARAM Act. Federal agencies, along with academic and international partners, are conducting work in almost every topical area identified in Section 12405 of the FOARAM Act and the subsequent draft research plan. The IWG-OA has identified all ongoing ocean acidification activities (Appendix 1) and is working with agency scientists and managers to coordinate future work. The IWG-OA is also working with domestic and international scientific advisory groups concerned with ocean acidification to ensure that the plan is well coordinated with non-government scientists and that it is informed by the latest scientific advice on ocean acidification. NSF and NOAA each contributed approximately $100,000 to underwrite the required review of this strategic research plan by the National Research Council.

Appendix 1: Summary of Federally Funded Ocean Acidification Research and Monitoring Activities

All agencies combined

Summary of funded ocean acidification research and monitoring activities			
	FY 2010 Budget ($K)	FY 2011 Budget ($K)	Activity Classification
1. Monitoring of ocean chemistry and biological impacts associated with ocean acidification.	$5,110	$4,887	Contributing
	$5,839	$6,425	Primary
	$10,949	$11,312	Total
2. Research to understand the species specific physiological responses of marine organisms to ocean acidification.	$2,180	$1,753	Contributing
	$20,432	$11,449	Primary
	$22,612	$13,202	Total
3. Modeling to predict changes in the ocean carbon cycle as a function of carbon dioxide and atmosphere-induced changes in temperature, ocean circulation, biogeochemistry, ecosystem and terrestrial input, and modeling to determine impacts on marine ecosystems and individual marine organisms.	$1,176	$838	Contributing
	$882	$831	Primary
	$2,058	$1,669	Total
4. Technology development and standardization of carbonate chemistry measurements on moorings and autonomous floats.	$306	$0	Contributing
	$1,160	$626	Primary
	$1,466	$626	Total
5. Assessment of socioeconomic impacts of ocean acidification an development of adaptation and mitigation strategies to conserve marine organisms and marine ecosystems	$0	$0	Contributing
	$157	$269	Primary
	$157	$269	Total
6. Education/Outreach on ocean acidification	$50	$0	Contributing
	$349	$392	Primary
	$399	$392	Total
7. Data Management and Integration	$75	$80	Contributing
	$100	$256	Primary
	$175	$336	Total
8. Other ocean acidification research and monitoring activities	$151	$151	Contributing
	$0	$515	Primary
	$151	$666	Total
	$9,048	$7,709	Total Contributing
	$28,919	$20,763	Total Primary
	$37,967	$28,472	Grand Total

Bureau of Ocean Energy Management

Summary of funded ocean acidification research and monitoring activities

Program Elements:

1. Monitoring of ocean chemistry and biological impacts associated with ocean acidification at selected coastal and open-ocean monitoring stations, including satellite-based monitoring to characterize marine ecosystems, changes in marine productivity, and changes in ocean chemistry.	FY 2010 Budget ($K)	FY 2011 Budget ($K)	Activity Classification
A) Marine Ecosystems			
Research in the Chukchi Sea on the current status of the ecosystem and its vulnerability to acidification as well as other aspects of climate change	$67	$200	Primary
Long-term monitoring at the East and West Flower Garden Banks in the Gulf of Mexico - Part of a 30 year effort to monitor the health of the coral reef, includes measurements of pH as a water quality parameter	$50	$45	Contributing
Monitoring of deepwater corals in the Gulf of Mexico in collaboration with NOAA	$1,000	$800	Contributing
B) Changes in marine productivity	$0	$0	
C) Changes in ocean chemistry	$0	$0	
	$1,050	**$845**	**Total Contributing**
	$67	**$200**	**Total Primary**
	$1,117	**$1,045**	**Total**
2. Research to understand the species specific physiological responses of marine organisms to ocean acidification, impacts on marine food webs from ocean acidification, and develop environmental and ecological indices that track marine ecosystem responses to ocean acidification.	FY 2010 Budget ($K)	FY 2011 Budget ($K)	Activity Classification
A) Biology of impacted species	$0	$0	
B) Ecosystems and Food Webs	$0	$0	
C) Calcification process and carbonate chemistry of the oceans	$0	$0	
D) Other marine chemical and physical effects	$0	$0	
E) The record of Earth system history re: ocean acidification	$0	$0	
3. Modeling to predict changes in the ocean carbon cycle as a function of carbon dioxide and atmosphere-induced changes in temperature, ocean circulation, biogeochemistry, ecosystem and terrestrial input, and modeling to determine impacts on marine ecosystems and individual marine organisms.	FY 2010 Budget ($K)	FY 2011 Budget ($K)	Activity Classification
A) Physico-chemical change	$0	$0	
B) Ecological/Biological impacts	$0	$0	
4. Technology development and standardization of carbonate chemistry measurements on moorings and autonomous floats.	$0	$0	

Bureau of Ocean Energy Management – continued

5. Assessment of socioeconomic impacts of ocean acidification an development of adaptation and mitigation strategies to conserve marine organisms and marine ecosystems	$0	$0	
6. Education/Outreach on ocean acidification	$0	$0	
7. Data Management and Integration	$0	$0	
8. Other ocean acidification research and monitoring activities	$0	$0	
	$1,050	$845	**Total Contributing**
	$67	$200	**Total Primary**
	$1,117	$1,045	**Grand Total**

Environmental Protection Agency

Summary of funded ocean acidification research and monitoring activities

Program Elements:

1. Monitoring of ocean chemistry and biological impacts associated with ocean acidification at selected coastal and open-ocean monitoring stations, including satellite-based monitoring to characterize marine ecosystems, changes in marine productivity, and changes in ocean chemistry.	FY 2010 Budget ($K)	FY 2011 Budget ($K)	Activity Classification
A) Marine Ecosystems			
Stony coral assessments conducted in Puerto Rico to document regional distribution and to test reef indicators for sensitivity to human disturbance	$2	$2	Contributing
Ecology and oceanography of harmful algal blooms	$18	$0	Contributing
B) Changes in marine productivity	$0	$0	
C) Changes in ocean chemistry	$0	$0	
	$20	**$2**	**Total Contributing**
	$0	**$0**	**Total Primary**
	$20	**$2**	**Total**
2. Research to understand the species specific physiological responses of marine organisms to ocean acidification, impacts on marine food webs from ocean acidification, and develop environmental and ecological indices that track marine ecosystem responses to ocean acidification.	FY 2010 Budget ($K)	FY 2011 Budget ($K)	Activity Classification
A) Biology of impacted species			
CO_2 effects on the demography of marine mysids	$0	$50	Primary
CO_2 effects on growth and food consumption by juvenile winter flounder	$0	$50	Primary
B) Ecosystems and Food Webs			
Preliminary study of CO2 effects on predator-prey interactions between juvenile winter flounder and marine mysids	$0	$10	Primary
C) Calcification process and carbonate chemistry of the oceans	$0	$0	
D) Other marine chemical and physical effects	$0	$0	
E) The record of Earth system history re: ocean acidification	$0	$0	
	$0	**$0**	**Total Contributing**
	$0	**$110**	**Total Primary**
	$0	**$110**	**Total**

Environmental Protection Agency – continued

	FY 2010 Budget ($K)	FY 2011 Budget ($K)	Activity Classification
3. Modeling to predict changes in the ocean carbon cycle as a function of carbon dioxide and atmosphere-induced changes in temperature, ocean circulation, biogeochemistry, ecosystem and terrestrial input, and modeling to determine impacts on marine ecosystems and individual marine organisms.	FY 2010 Budget ($K)	FY 2011 Budget ($K)	Activity Classification
A) Physico-chemical change	$0	$0	
B) Ecological/Biological impacts			
Modeling and projecting ecological impacts of ocean acidification using inverse demographic techniques	$0	$50	Primary
	$0	**$0**	**Total Contributing**
	$0	**$50**	**Total Primary**
	$0	**$50**	**Total**
4. Technology development and standardization of carbonate chemistry measurements on moorings and autonomous floats.	$0	$0	
5. Assessment of socioeconomic impacts of ocean acidification an development of adaptation and mitigation strategies to conserve marine organisms and marine ecosystems	FY 2010 Budget ($K)	FY 2011 Budget ($K)	Activity Classification
Developing integrated assessment models	$150	$200	Primary
Economic analysis of COMBO model outputs	$0	$25	Primary
	$0	**$0**	**Total Contributing**
	$150	**$225**	**Total Primary**
	$150	**$225**	**Total**
6. Education/Outreach on ocean acidification	$0	$0	
7. Data Management and Integration	$0	$0	
8. Other ocean acidification research and monitoring activities	$0	$0	
	$20	**$2**	**Total Contributing**
	$150	**$385**	**Total Primary**
	$170	**$387**	**Grand Total**

National Aeronautics and Space Administration

Summary of funded ocean acidification research and monitoring activities

1. Monitoring of ocean chemistry and biological impacts associated with ocean acidification at selected coastal and open-ocean monitoring stations, including satellite-based monitoring to characterize marine ecosystems, changes in marine productivity, and changes in ocean chemistry.		FY 2010 Budget ($K)	FY 2011 Budget ($K)	Activity Classification
A) Marine Ecosystems B) Changes in marine productivity C) Changes in ocean chemistry	NASA has a fleet of Earth Observing satellites whose data are used for research. Not operationally monitoring observations.	$0	$0	

2. Research to understand the species specific physiological responses of marine organisms to ocean acidification, impacts on marine food webs from ocean acidification, and develop environmental and ecological indices that track marine ecosystem responses to ocean acidification.		FY 2010 Budget ($K)	FY 2011 Budget ($K)	Activity Classification
A) Biology of impacted species B) Ecosystems and Food Webs C) Calcification process and carbonate chemistry of the oceans D) Other marine chemical and physical effects E) The record of Earth system history re: ocean acidification	Studies to determining properties of the ocean related to ocean acidity and the impacts of ocean acidification on ocean ecosystems, ICESCAPES program, and, global scale assessments of primary production.	$2,292	$2,177	Primary
		$0	$0	**Total Contributing**
		$2,292	**$2,177**	**Total Primary**
		$2,292	**$2,177**	**Total**

3. Modeling to predict changes in the ocean carbon cycle as a function of carbon dioxide and atmosphere-induced changes in temperature, ocean circulation, biogeochemistry, ecosystem and terrestrial input, and modeling to determine impacts on marine ecosystems and individual marine organisms.		FY 2010 Budget ($K)	FY 2011 Budget ($K)	Activity Classification
A) Physico-chemical change B) Ecological/Biological Impacts	Modeling of ocean acidification within the greater Caribbean, Method development for predicting coastal surface-water pCO_2 from remote-sensing data.	$657	$540	Primary
		$0	$0	**Total Contributing**
		$657	**$540**	**Total Primary**
		$657	**$540**	**Total**

National Aeronautics and Space Administration – continued

4. Technology development and standardization of carbonate chemistry measurements on moorings and autonomous floats.	FY 2010 Budget ($K)	FY 2011 Budget ($K)	Activity Classification
Development, assessment, and commercialization of a biogeochemical profiling float for ocean carbon studies	$265	$0	Primary
	$0	$0	**Total Contributing**
	$265	**$0**	**Total Primary**
	$265	**$0**	**Total**
5. Assessment of socioeconomic impacts of ocean acidification an development of adaptation and mitigation strategies to conserve marine organisms and marine ecosystems	$0	$0	
6. Education/Outreach on ocean acidification	FY 2010 Budget ($K)	FY 2011 Budget ($K)	Activity Classification
Funded awards for improving the interface between scientific research and education	$100	$100	Primary
	$0	$0	**Total Contributing**
	$100	**$100**	**Total Primary**
	$100	**$100**	**Total**
7. Data Management and Integration	$0	$0	
8. Other ocean acidification research and monitoring activities	$0	$0	
	$0	$0	**Total Contributing**
	$3,314	**$2,817**	**Total Primary**
	$3,314	**$2,817**	**Grand Total**

National Oceanic and Atmospheric Administration

Summary of funded ocean acidification research and monitoring activities			
Program Elements			
1. Monitoring of ocean chemistry and biological impacts associated with ocean acidification at selected coastal and open-ocean monitoring stations, including satellite-based monitoring to characterize marine ecosystems, changes in marine productivity, and changes in ocean chemistry.	FY 2010 Budget ($K)	FY 2011 Budget ($K)	Activity Classification
A) Marine Ecosystems			
Atlantic Ocean Acidification Test-bed	$300	$310	Primary
Coral-based Proxy Records of Ocean Acidification: A Pilot Study at the Puerto Rico Test-bed Site	$65	$0	Primary
Coral Growth and Reef Framework Persistence of the Florida Reef Tract with Accelerating Ocean Acidification	$45	$125	Primary
Ocean Acidification – Calcification Rates of Corals and Crustose Coraline Algae in the Pacific Islands	$190	$50	Primary
Ocean acidification - Spatial and Temporal Patterns of Carbonate Chemistry in the Pacific Islands	$100	$100	Primary
Climate Change Impacts: Potential for Recovery/Resilience of Corals and Algal Interference	$0	$125	Primary
NOAA Pacific Islands Fisheries Science Center (PIFSC) Ocean Acidification Research Implementation Plan for FY11	$0	$180	Primary
B) Changes in marine productivity	$0	$0	
C) Changes in ocean chemistry			
NOAA Ocean, Coastal, and Estuary OA Monitoring Network: Pacific, West Coast; Atlantic, Caribbean, Gulf of Mexico	$3,736	$4,033	Primary
NOAA Climate Observation Division: Repeat hydrography, underway pCO_2 and moored pCO_2	$3,150	$3,150	Contributing
	$3,150	**$3,150**	**Total Contributing**
	$4,436	**$4,923**	**Total Primary**
	$7,586	**$8,073**	**Total**
2. Research to understand the species specific physiological responses of marine organisms to ocean acidification, impacts on marine food webs from ocean acidification, and develop environmental and ecological indices that track marine ecosystem responses to ocean acidification.	FY 2010 Budget ($K)	FY 2011 Budget ($K)	Activity Classification
A) Biology of impacted species **B) Ecosystems and Food Webs** **C) Calcification process and carbonate chemistry of the oceans** **D) Other marine chemical and physical effects** **E) The record of Earth system history re: ocean acidification** — NOAA Fisheries Science Center Ocean Acidification Species Response Research, this project spans all sections A-E.	$1,207	$1,348	Primary

	$0	$0	Total Contributing
	$1,207	**$1,348**	**Total Primary**
	$1,207	**$1,348**	**Total**
3. Modeling to predict changes in the ocean carbon cycle as a function of carbon dioxide and atmosphere-induced changes in temperature, ocean circulation, biogeochemistry, ecosystem and terrestrial input, and modeling to determine impacts on marine ecosystems and individual marine organisms.	FY 2010 Budget ($K)	FY 2011 Budget ($K)	Activity Classification
A) Physico-chemical change			
Shallow Water Hypoxia – Tipping the Balance for Individuals, Populations and Ecosystems; Impacts on Oysters and Fish	$634	$62	Contributing
Development and testing of algorithms for various regions for application of other standard oceanographic measurements to OA	$200	$200	Contributing
B) Ecological/Biological Impacts			
Modeling impacts on commercially important species in AK, Northeast, and Northwest US	$114	$130	Primary
	$834	**$262**	**Total Contributing**
	$114	**$130**	**Total Primary**
	$948	**$392**	**Total**
4. Technology development and standardization of carbonate chemistry measurements on moorings and autonomous floats.	FY 2010 Budget ($K)	FY 2011 Budget ($K)	Activity Classification
Observing systems: gliders	$0	$340	Primary
Physical and Biogeochemical Processes Controlling Temporal Variability in Ocean Acidification at Conch Reef, Florida	$0	$75	Primary
Disolved Inorganic Carbon Sensor development for use on moorings	$100	$100	Primary
	$0	**$0**	**Total Contributing**
	$100	**$515**	**Total Primary**
	$100	**$515**	**Total**
5. Assessment of socioeconomic impacts of ocean acidification an development of adaptation and mitigation strategies to conserve marine organisms and marine ecosystems	FY 2010 Budget ($K)	FY 2011 Budget ($K)	Activity Classification
Development of a model in Alaska to relate effects of OA on Alaska King Crab to the potential economic impacts	$7	$44	Primary

	$0	$0	**Total Contributing**
	$7	$44	**Total Primary**
	$7	$44	**Total**
6. Education/Outreach on ocean acidification	FY 2010 Budget ($K)	FY 2011 Budget ($K)	Activity Classification
NWFSC Education & Outreach	$12	$23	Primary
NOAA Education Office Ocean Acidification Education and Outreach	$44	$44	Primary
NMFSC OA Workshop	$43	$0	Primary
Coral Reef Ocean Acidification Monitoring Portfolio Workshop	$0	$50	Primary
Workshop to Develop a Comprehensive Interagency Ocean Acidification Data Management Plan	$0	$50	Primary
International Workshop to Develop an Ocean Acidification Observing Network of Ship Surveys, Moorings, Floats, and Gliders.	$0	$125	Primary
	$0	$0	**Total Contributing**
	$99	$292	**Total Primary**
	$99	$292	**Total**
7. Data Management and Integration (specific projects where data management was the main focus, projects listed under other themes include the cost of managing that data)	FY 2010 Budget ($K)	FY 2011 Budget ($K)	Activity Classification
Data coordination, management and product development	$100	$206	Primary
Interagency Ocean Acidification Data Management Workshop	$0	$50	Primary
	$0	$0	**Total Contributing**
	$100	$256	**Total Primary**
	$100	$256	**Total**
8. Other ocean acidification research and monitoring activities	FY 2010 Budget ($K)	FY 2011 Budget ($K)	Activity Classification
NOAA Ocean Acidification Program Office	$0	$253	Primary
Review of the Strategic Research Plan	$0	$106	Primary
	$0	$0	**Total Contributing**
	$0	$359	**Total Primary**
	$0	$359	**Total**
	$3,984	$3,412	**Total Contributing**
	$6,063	$7,867	**Total Primary**
	$10,047	$11,279	**Grand Total**

National Science Foundation

Summary of funded ocean acidification research and monitoring activities

Program Elements:

1. Monitoring of ocean chemistry and biological impacts associated with ocean acidification at selected coastal and open-ocean monitoring stations, including satellite-based monitoring to characterize marine ecosystems, changes in marine productivity, and changes in ocean chemistry.	FY 2010 Budget ($K)	FY 2011 Budget ($K)	Activity Classification
A) Marine Ecosystems			
Ocean time series monitoring - Species	$230	$230	Contributing
B) Changes in marine productivity			
Ocean Time series - Productivity	$230	$230	Contributing
C) Changes in ocean chemistry			
Ocean time series monitoring - Chemistry	$430	$430	Contributing
Bering Strait time series	$100	$100	Primary
	$890	**$890**	**Total Contributing**
	$100	**$100**	**Total Primary**
	$990	**$990**	**Total**
2. Research to understand the species specific physiological responses of marine organisms to ocean acidification, impacts on marine food webs from ocean acidification, and develop environmental and ecological indices that track marine ecosystem responses to ocean acidification.	FY 2010 Budget ($K)	FY 2011 Budget ($K)	Activity Classification
A) Biology of impacted species			
pH changes in estuarine systems and effects on organisms with $CaCO_3$ exoskeleton	$1,372	$691	Contributing
Interactive effects of temperature, nutrients and pH on coral physiology and calcification	$10,456	$7,740	Primary
B) Ecosystems and Food Webs			
Changes in protists community structure with increased CO_2 and temperature; effects of iron availability on phytoplankton composition in high pH water	$355	$476	Contributing
Effects of pCO2 and pH on Photosynthesis, Respiration and Growth in Marine Phytoplankton; physiological effects of pCO_2 on larvae development of benthic organism	$1,952	$0	Primary
C) Calcification process and carbonate chemistry of the oceans			
Effects/controls on seasonal hypoxia and acidification	$0	$133	Contributing
Develop global surface ocean baseline for pH; physical and biogeochemical processes on carbonate minerals in the Western Arctic; changes in the carbonate pump; calcification in low saturation seawater; characterize spatial and temporal variability in pH and carbonate chemistry along the Pacific coast	$2,237	$0	Primary

National Science Foundation – continued

	FY 2010 Budget ($K)	FY 2011 Budget ($K)	Activity Classification
D) Other marine chemical and physical effects Acclimatization or adaptation capacity of calcifying invertebrates to increased pH; fate of organic matter	$1,299	$0	Primary
E) The record of Earth system history re: ocean acidification Ocean acidification proxies and the marine sediment record; analysis of boron isotope seawater-pH indicator in deep-water corals	$915	$0	Primary
	$1,727	**$1,300**	**Total Contributing**
	$16,859	**$7,740**	**Total Primary**
	$18,586	**$9,040**	**Total**
3. Modeling to predict changes in the ocean carbon cycle as a function of carbon dioxide and atmosphere-induced changes in temperature, ocean circulation, biogeochemistry, ecosystem and terrestrial input, and modeling to determine impacts on marine ecosystems and individual marine organisms.	FY 2010 Budget ($K)	FY 2011 Budget ($K)	Activity Classification
A) Physico-chemical change Observationally-based analysis of past and future transport of anthropogenic CO_2 in the ocean	$0	$234	Contributing
B) Ecological/Biological Impacts	$0	$0	
	$0	**$234**	**Total Contributing**
	$0	**$0**	**Total Primary**
	$0	**$234**	**Total**
4. Technology development and standardization of carbonate chemistry measurements on moorings and autonomous floats.	FY 2010 Budget ($K)	FY 2011 Budget ($K)	Activity Classification
Development of a micro-rosette sensor for total dissolved inorganic carbon from autonomous profiler	$306	$0	Contributing
Development of instrumentation to control seawater composition; quality control of oceanic carbon dioxide measurements	$684	$0	Primary
	$306	**$0**	**Total Contributing**
	$684	**$0**	**Total Primary**
	$990	**$0**	**Total**
5. Assessment of socioeconomic impacts of ocean acidification an development of adaptation and mitigation strategies to conserve marine organisms and marine ecosystems	$0	$0	

National Science Foundation – continued

6. Education/Outreach on ocean acidification	FY 2010 Budget ($K)	FY 2011 Budget ($K)	Activity Classification
Symposium on The Ocean in a High-CO2 World	$50	$0	Contributing
	$50	**$0**	**Total Contributing**
	$0	**$0**	**Total Primary**
	$50	**$0**	**Total**

7. Data Management and Integration	FY 2010 Budget ($K)	FY 2011 Budget ($K)	Activity Classification
Biological and Chemical Oceanography Data Management Office (BCO-DMO)	$75	$80	Contributing
	$75	**$80**	**Total Contributing**
	$0	**$0**	**Total Primary**
	$75	**$80**	**Total**

8. Other ocean acidification research and monitoring activities	FY 2010 Budget ($K)	FY 2011 Budget ($K)	Activity Classification
Renovations marine science laboratory at USF	$63	$63	Contributing
Renovations marine science observing systems at UMCES	$88	$88	Contributing
Ocean acidification Principal Investigators' meeting; review of the National Ocean Acidification Research and Monitoring Plan	$0	$156	Primary
	$151	**$151**	**Total Contributing**
	$0	**$156**	**Total Primary**
	$151	**$307**	**Total**
	$3,199	**$2,655**	**Total Contributing**
	$17,643	**$7,996**	**Total Primary**
	$20,842	**$10,651**	**Grand Total**

U.S. Geological Survey - Number in parentheses indicates it is a project that spans a number of program elements. A number is then indicated in subsequent cells, but $ numbers are not; blank cells indicate a component of a larger project that has an interface with ocean acidification, but unsure how to tease out exact dollar amounts.

Summary of funded ocean acidification research and monitoring activities			
Program Elements:			
1. Monitoring of ocean chemistry and biological impacts associated with ocean acidification at selected coastal and open-ocean monitoring stations, including satellite-based monitoring to characterize marine ecosystems, changes in marine productivity, and changes in ocean chemistry.	FY 2010 Budget ($K)	FY 2011 Budget ($K)	Activity Classification
A) Marine Ecosystems			
In situ measurement of coral reef community metabolism and calcification baselines and thresholds of pCO_2, pH, and sat. state for calcification and dissolution	$377 [1]	$377 [1]	Primary
Provides baseline information on the latitudinal and seasonal variability in calcification rates for a species of reef-building coral and encrusting coralline algal communities throughout the Florida Keys	$255 [3]	$255 [3]	Primary
Utilizes historical information, field work, and satellite data to understand the response of Florida Shelf Ecosystems to climate change	$514 [2]	$490 [2]	Primary
B) Changes in marine productivity			
In situ measurement of coral reef community metabolism and calcification baselines and thresholds of pCO_2, pH, and sat. state for calcification and dissolution	[1]	[1]	Primary
C) Changes in ocean chemistry			
Coastal and shelf Florida waters: utilizes historical information, field work and satellite data to understand the response of Florida Shelf Ecosystems to climate change	[2]	[2]	Primary
Links between water chemistry, geology, and biologic communities: data synthesis of collected WFS data including, pCO_2 (seawater and atmosphere), total carbon, pH, DIC, temperature and salinity.	[2]	[2]	Primary
Arctic ocean - ocean acidification: key baseline data on pCO2 (seawater and atmosphere), total carbon, pH, DIC, temperature and salinity in waters of the Arctic- with LOS	$90	$80	Primary
Diurnal changes in coastal carbonate chemistry: measuring diurnal changes in coastal and reef	[1]	[1]	Primary
	$0	$0	**Total Contributing**
	$1,236	$1,202	**Total Primary**
	$1,236	$1,202	**Total**

U.S. Geological Survey – continued

2. Research to understand the species specific physiological responses of marine organisms to ocean acidification, impacts on marine food webs from ocean acidification, and develop environmental and ecological indices that track marine ecosystem responses to ocean acidification.	FY 2010 Budget ($K)	FY 2011 Budget ($K)	Activity Classification
A) Biology of impacted species			
Coral Reef degradation including coralline algae: study on encrusting coralline algal communities on coral reefs.	$74	$74	Primary
Identifying and characterizing microbial communities associated with the cold-water coral Lophelia pertusa as a baseline for biology and ecology of this deep-reef habitat-former.	$217	$217	Contributing
Laboratory experiments to evaluate the effects of lower pH and saturation state on calcifying organisms and is part of dissertation research of University of South Florida student	[2]	[2]	Primary
Examine benthic community structure and trophic function in deep-coral ecosystems in the Gulf of Mexico- response to change			Contributing
B) Ecosystems and Food Webs	$0	$0	
C) Calcification process and carbonate chemistry of the oceans	$0	$0	
D) Other marine chemical and physical effects			
Numerical modeling of flow patterns and discharge rates to Biscayne Bay to provide insight into causes of ecosystem degradation	$55	$55	Contributing
Quantifying flux in groundwater nutrients to the coastal ocean and coral reef settings in Hawaii with expected climate change.			Contributing
E) The record of Earth system history re: ocean acidification			
Determine baseline data on the seasonal variability in calcification rates for a species of reef-building coral and encrusting coralline algal communities in Dry Tortugas National Park	$181	$181	Contributing
Chronic effects on the growth rates of coral and macroalgae: effects on algal growth rates and coral growth and recruitment	[3]	[3]	Primary
Synthesis of Historical data from Florida's shellfish beds to document ocean acidification and climate change	[2]	[2]	Primary
Coral Reef Community Calcification: examines past, current, and future calcification rates relative to changes in ocean chemistry	[1]	[1]	Primary
	$453	**$453**	**Total Contributing**
	$74	**$74**	**Total Primary**
	$527	**$527**	**Total**

U.S. Geological Survey - continued

3. Modeling to predict changes in the ocean carbon cycle as a function of carbon dioxide and atmosphere-induced changes in temperature, ocean circulation, biogeochemistry, ecosystem and terrestrial input, and modeling to determine impacts on marine ecosystems and individual marine organisms.	FY 2010 Budget ($K)	FY 2011 Budget ($K)	Activity Classification
A) Physico-chemical change			
Modeling carbon fluxes (ocean and aquatic): integrating existing information; Carbon fluxes in hydrologic and geologic processes	$342	$342	Contributing
Modeling historical and future changes in ocean carbon cycle: using boron proxy on coral cores and data from present day reefs, modeling ecosystem change	$111	$111	Primary
Determine whether Arctic gas hydrates are currently contributing or can reasonably be expected to contribute (under accepted climate change scenarios) to methane seepage offshore Alaska or in areas of continuous permafrost on the Alaskan North Slope			Contributing
B) Ecological/Biological Impacts			
Examine the link between iron solubility and speciation in particulate sources of Alaskan waters, and the connection to marine productivity, carbon sequestration and global change (OA)			Contributing
Yukon River Basin and the North Slope: defining the spatial distributions and fluxes of carbon stocks in various biological and chemical forms and the biogeochemical mechanisms controlling these carbon fluxes			Contributing
Quantify Ecosystem Performance anomalies for North Slope, AK; expedite eMODIS data			Contributing
	$342	**$342**	**Total Contributing**
	$111	**$111**	**Total Primary**
	$453	**$453**	**Total**
4. Technology development and standardization of carbonate chemistry measurements on moorings and autonomous floats.	FY 2010 Budget ($K)	FY 2011 Budget ($K)	Activity Classification
Development of Boron isotopes as a proxy for seawater pH	$111	$111	Primary
Methods for measuring Coral Reef Community metabolism and calcification: standardization of methods measuring carbon parameters and calcification; partnering with NOAA, USF, RSMAS, USGS	[1]	[1]	Primary
	$0	**$0**	**Total Contributing**
	$111	**$111**	**Total Primary**
	$111	**$111**	**Total**

5. Assessment of socioeconomic impacts of ocean acidification an development of adaptation and mitigation strategies to conserve marine organisms and marine ecosystems	$0	$0	
6. Education/Outreach on ocean acidification	FY 2010 Budget ($K)	FY 2011 Budget ($K)	Activity Classification
Various outreach associated with projects; Soundwaves articles	1,2,3, etc	1,2,3, etc	Contributing
7. Data Management and Integration	$0	$0	
8. Other ocean acidification research and monitoring activities	FY 2010 Budget ($K)	FY 2011 Budget ($K)	Activity Classification
USGS Carbon Committee: leadership for USGS Interdisciplinary Carbon Committee			Contributing
Membership on SOLAS-IMBER, OCB-OA: leadership for international and national committees	[2]	[2]	Contributing
	$795	$795	**Total Contributing**
	$1,532	$1,498	**Total Primary**
	$2,327	$2,293	**Grand Total**

Number in parentheses indicates it is a project that spans a number of program elements. Number is then indicated in subsequent cells, but $ numbers are not; blank cells indicate a component of a larger project that has an interface with ocean acidification, but unsure how to tease out exact dollar amounts.